Standard® PUBLISHING
Bringing the Word to Life™
Cincinnati, Ohio

Published by Standard Publishing, Cincinnati, Ohio
www.standardpub.com

Copyright © 2008 Standard Publishing

Printed in: USA
Project editor: Kelly Carr
Cover and interior design: The DesignWorks Group

ISBN 978-0-7847-2245-9

14 13 12 11 10 09 08   9 8 7 6 5 4 3 2 1

CONTENTS

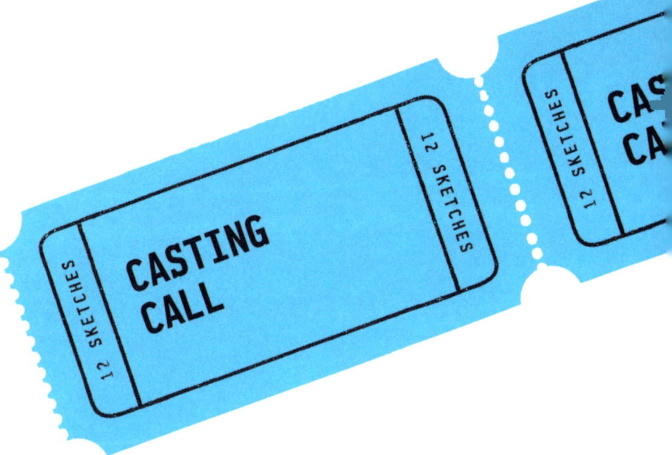

We're glad you picked up this book. The sketches take important Bible topics and introduce them from unique, current perspectives. There are parodies of popular culture as well as realistic teen situations to draw students into the action.

Stories resonate with students. By constructing modern-day stories from topics in the Bible, the ideas will capture teens' attention and stick in their minds. Those acting out the skits as well as those watching will realize that the topics found in God's Word truly ARE relevant to their daily lives!

We all know students who have a dramatic flair for life. That's who we had in mind when we created these skits. Each skit is designed for teens to use their skills in dramatizing issues discussed in the Bible that also remain relevant to their lives today. These skits are limited—in a good way: limited to a few cast members, a few lines to learn, and a few props.

So whether you are kicking off your youth group time, opening a retreat session, beginning a Sunday school lesson, or introducing a sermon, the skits in this book will get your teens in on the act!

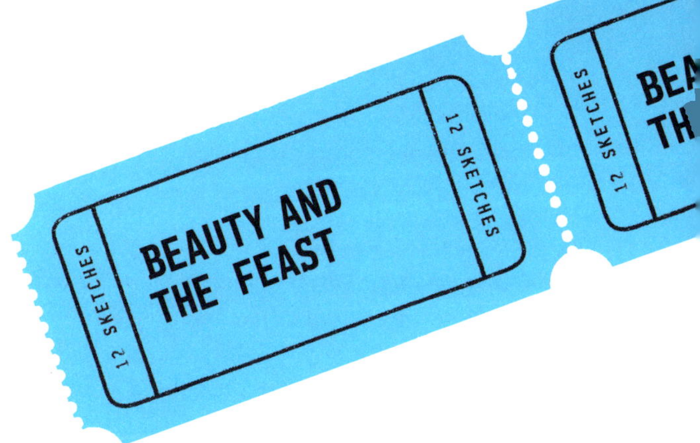

Use this fractured fable to introduce a discussion about hypocrisy and being a sincere follower of Jesus.

Matthew 21:18-22

Luke 11:37-46

storybook

picket sign or poster saying "Don't eat meat! Animals are sweet!" on one side and "Don't go! There's BO!" on the other side

(optional) two small packages wrapped in white paper to look like meat from a butcher; one should have "tasty pork chops" written on it and another, "beef nuggets."

(optional) hamburger

Narrator

Alice

Sam

Director

Extras (two)—nonspeaking roles

Begin with Narrator *standing to the front of the stage, off to one side.* Narrator *is holding a storybook and speaks as if reading a fairy tale to the audience. Picket sign should lie flat on stage floor, unnoticeable to audience.*

Narrator: Once upon a time there lived a beautiful vegetarian named Alice.

*[*Alice *hops out on stage and waves to audience.]*

Alice: Hi!

Narrator: Now Alice loved animals of all kinds—cows, pigs, chickens, and sheep.

*[*Alice *walks around the stage, pretending to pet animals.]*

Narrator: She named every cow she ever met. Lovable names like Mugsy and Burt.

Alice: *[pretending to talk to a cow]* Hmm, you look like a Gerty to me.

Narrator: Not only did Alice abstain from eating any kind of meat, she was diabolically opposed to other people who didn't mind a juicy steak now and then. In fact, she made quite a nuisance of herself. She would picket local burger restaurants.

*[*Alice *picks up the picket sign/poster, with the "Animals are sweet!" side facing the audience, and marches. She keeps picketing through her and* Narrator's *next line.]*

Alice: *[chants]* Don't eat meat! Animals are sweet!

Narrator: A couple of times, she chained herself to the Dog and Suds hot dog cart. At the town steakhouse, she even painted the giant cow atop their restaurant completely black, with red letters reading "Cow of Death."

Alice: *[stops picketing and looks at* Narrator*]* Hey, you don't need to make me sound like such a grump! *[puts down picket sign]*

NARRATOR: One day, while walking downtown, she noticed two people emerging from a shop.

[EXTRAS walk onto the stage, carrying their packages (or pretending to carry packages), cross stage, and exit off the other side by the time ALICE says her next line.]

NARRATOR: Both were carrying white packages in their arms. One read "tasty pork chops"; another read "beef nuggets." Alice was appalled!

ALICE: *[calling out to the EXTRAS]* What's going on here?!

NARRATOR: She screamed.

ALICE: *[looks at NARRATOR]* Screamed?

NARRATOR: OK. Yelled?

ALICE: I don't think so.

NARRATOR: She calmly said in a polite and ladylike way.

ALICE: Much better!

NARRATOR: Alice knew what she had to do. *[emphasize the p-words in this sentence]* She went to the butcher shop from where the people with packages were parading.

[ALICE now pretends to see the butcher shop and gets her picket sign/poster as NARRATOR says his next line. She turns the sign so that the "BO" side faces the audience.]

NARRATOR: Then Alice stood in front of the shop window with her sign and yelled—

ALICE: Excuse me?

NARRATOR: And said *sweetly* to passersby . . .

[EXTRAS walk back onto the stage and walk toward ALICE and the shop. When she says the next line, EXTRAS shriek and run away from the shop.]

ALICE: *[sweetly yells]* Whatever you do, don't go inside this shop. Someone in there has really bad BO!

NARRATOR: People shrieked and ran away in horror. Hours passed, and not a single customer entered the shop. A shop that usually did a significant amount of business. Finally, a tall, dark, and stunningly handsome man—

[SAM peeks out from backstage to say next line.]

SAM: Why, thank you!

[SAM retreats.]

NARRATOR: Don't mention it. A tall, dark, and stunningly handsome man came out of the store. At once, Alice melted under his spell.

[SAM enters.]

SAM: Ma'am, uh, I don't mean to complain, but why are you in front of my shop yellin' about BO?

NARRATOR: Alice stammered, unable to keep a reasonable thought in her head. Which actually wasn't unusual.

ALICE: *[to NARRATOR]* Hey! I heard that!

NARRATOR: The wheel is spinning but the hamster is dead, if you know what I mean.

ALICE: *[to NARRATOR]* All right! I've just about had it with you!

SAM: Hey. Can we just get back to this scene? I got a date tonight.

ALICE: With who?

SAM: Your sister.

ALICE: What?

[DIRECTOR comes out on stage.]

DIRECTOR: Cut, cut. Sam, that's the *Days of Our Lives* skit.

SAM: Oh, right. My mistake.

DIRECTOR: All right. 3, 2, 1, and ACTION! *[exits stage]*

ALICE: Wow! You sure are tall, dark, and stunningly handsome!

SAM: That's what the script says! Hey, do you like burgers?

ALICE: Um . . .

NARRATOR: At this, Alice was conflicted. All her beliefs were being challenged by this hunk of a guy. Which would she choose, the cute boy or the principles she'd stood by her entire life?

[SAM smiles brightly to persuade ALICE.]

ALICE: Um . . .

NARRATOR: You already said that. We're waiting.

ALICE: I've always loved animals. But Sam is REALLY cute!

NARRATOR: And so Alice made her choice. The two star-crossed loves went for a late-night walk, strolling through the thick moonlight, nibbling on a burger for two.

[SAM and ALICE walk with arms linked, sharing (or pretending to eat) a hamburger.]

SAM: Do you believe in love at first sight?

ALICE: Only if it's a love between a girl and her bacon double cheeseburger!

NARRATOR: Alice popped the last cheesy morsel into her mouth. Oh sure, the cows look at her differently now, but she looks at them differently too. And they all lived happily ever after. Well, everyone but Mugsy, Burt, and Gerty. The end. *[closes storybook]*

[DIRECTOR steps back on stage and says last line to audience.]

DIRECTOR: No animals were killed or injured in the reading of this skit.

Use this skit to introduce a discussion about respect and how it can improve relationships (especially dating relationships).

Ruth 2–4

Romans 13:8

1 Corinthians 10:24

1 Peter 3:7

two backpacks

cell phone

Todd

Seth

Todd and Seth have backpacks on and can walk together, as if exiting school. They should stop near the middle to front of stage when Seth starts texting.

Todd: That English test was awful. What a way to end the day.

Seth: I know. Shakespeare fried my brain.

Todd: Hey, I think I'm gonna ask Shondra to go to the baseball game with me tomorrow night. Do you think she'd say yes?

Seth: Hold on and I'll find out. *[pulls cell phone out of pocket and begins to text]*

Todd: Seth, what are you doing?

Seth: I'm texting Natalie to ask her if she thinks Shondra would say yes.

Todd: Will Natalie know what Shondra would say?

Seth: Of course. Todd, don't you know girls talk to their friends about *everything*?!

Todd: About *everything*? Great. What if they *both* laugh at me behind my back?

Seth: You'll be fine. *[As he types, he reads his text out loud to Todd, speaking a little slower than normal since he's supposed to be typing at the same time.]* Hey, Natalie. Todd says Shondra is cute. Think she'd go out with him?

Todd: Dude, you weren't even subtle!

Seth: You don't have time for subtle. Do you want to know or do you want to know?

Todd: You're right.

Seth: Look, Natalie wrote back.

Todd: What'd she say? What'd she say? *[looks over Seth's shoulder to see phone screen]*

Seth: *[reading]* "Tell Todd Shondra would say yes."

Todd: Cool.

Seth: Wait. She sent another text. *[reading]* "Tell him if Shondra's busy, I know someone who could keep him company. Wink. Wink."

Todd: What? Is Natalie hitting on me?

Seth: I think so! And Natalie's hotter than Shondra.

Todd: Seth, that's wrong, and you know it. Natalie is *supposed* to be dating Miguel. I couldn't do that to a friend.

Seth: You're right. I know. I shouldn't have said that. Wait, Natalie texted me something else. *[reading]* "Tell Todd that Miguel is out of town this weekend." Man, she's trying hard!

Todd: Too hard. Girls like that are dangerous.

Seth: Doesn't it make you feel just a little bit better about yourself, knowing a girl *that* good-looking is flirting with you?

Todd: At first, maybe. But in the long run, it means she's bad news. Why don't some girls understand that acting that way doesn't make them attractive? At least not to the right kind of guys.

Seth: Yeah.

Todd: Do you think Shondra's like that too? If so, I don't want to go out with her.

Seth: Just because she's friends with Natalie doesn't mean she's exactly like her. Just be honest with Shondra and tell her that you're interested in going out—but not if she acts like Natalie.

Todd: Yeah, I guess being honest with her is the best way to go.

Seth: What should I text back to Natalie?

Todd: Here. Give me your phone. *[texting]* "Hey, it's Todd. Tell Shondra I'll call her later. And I don't mess around with my friends' girlfriends." Well, Seth, I guess there's only one thing left to do.

Seth: What's that?

Todd: Go talk to Miguel when he gets back in town. He needs a new girl who will treat him with respect.

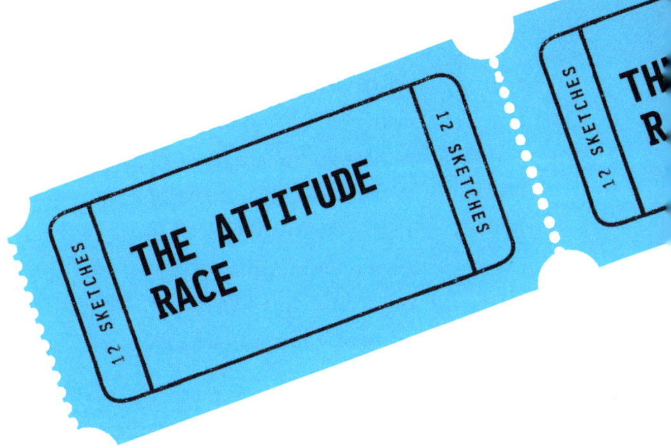

Use this parody of *The Amazing Race* to introduce a discussion about productive ways to handle conflict.

Matthew 18:15-18

Acts 6:1-7

stool

piece of yellow paper to represent a race clue

map

two chairs

(optional) table

(optional) two plates of breakfast food with forks and napkins

FRANK—host of *The Attitude Race* (may use a British/Australian accent to imitate *The Amazing Race* TV host)

Heather—sister and teammate of Michelle; needs to have blonde hair or else alter the blonde comment about her in the script

Michelle—sister and teammate of Heather

Craig—best friend and teammate of Ben

Ben—best friend and teammate of Craig

Uriah—husband and teammate of Joy

Joy—wife and teammate of Uriah

Extras (need two)—nonspeaking roles

Frank sits on front side of stage on a stool the whole time to narrate and watches the action when he isn't talking. All three pairs will enter from the same side of stage and exit off the other side of the stage. Then when they return for their second scenes, they will enter from that opposite side and exit at the original places.

Frank: Welcome to *The Attitude Race.* The three remaining teams are in Paris . . . Paris, Kentucky, that is—their tenth stop in a race across the country. Heather and Michelle, the two sisters, were the first to arrive at the pit stop last night and will leave at 6:00 AM. Their first clue leads them to a local diner.

[Heather and Michelle run out on stage, reading their clue.]

Heather: Look at the clue, Michelle. It says, *[emphasize italicized words]* "Listen to your favorite jukebox *tune* at this famous greasy *spoon*."

Michelle: OK. Let's grab a taxi and find some famous diner.

Heather: Are you sure that's where we go?

Michelle: *[sarcastic]* Hello, Heather! "Jukebox tune" and "greasy spoon"? That's definitely a diner. You are such a blonde!

Heather: Hey! My hair is dyed, thank you very much.

Michelle: *[sarcastic] That's* something to brag about.

[Heather and Michelle run offstage.]

Frank: Best friends Craig and Ben get to set out at 6:30 AM. The husband and wife team of Uriah and Joy follow close behind at 6:40. Both teams head to find the famous diner here in town. Craig and Ben find some locals and ask about the clue.

[CRAIG and BEN walk out on stage, looking at a map. They approach the front of the stage.]

CRAIG: *[pointing into audience as if he's seen some local citizens; speaks hopefully]* Ben, let's ask these people. They might be able to help.

BEN: *[abrupt and slightly rude]* Hey, we're looking for a famous local diner. Do you know it? How do you get there? *[pauses for a moment then says to CRAIG in frustration]* Craig, these people don't know where it is. This is a waste of our time!

CRAIG: *[embarrassed and whispers]* Ben! They can hear you! Be nice!

BEN: *[to CRAIG]* We're never going to see these people again. What's the problem? *[then to audience again as if to the locals]* Could you hurry up a bit? We're in a race!

[CRAIG and BEN exit.]

FRANK: Uriah and Joy had talked to their cab driver. He knew the famous diner called The Roost and quickly took them there.

[URIAH and JOY enter, walking across the stage toward opposite side of stage as they talk.]

URIAH: Joy, I'm so glad our cab driver knew the diner. We got here in no time!

JOY: Good job, Uriah! I knew if we stayed patient and stayed positive, we'd do well in the race!

[URIAH and JOY exit.]

FRANK: Craig and Ben figured out that the diner they needed was The Roost and found their way there, seeing that Heather and Michelle and Uriah and Joy had already arrived. Once at The Roost, teams encountered a detour. A detour is a choice between two tasks, each with its own pros and cons. This detour is called Gorge or Forge. If teams choose Gorge, they must sit down at The Roost and eat seven plates of the restaurant's signature breakfast dish: the Sunrise Sampler. This task may seem great to a hungry person, but all teams started off their morning with a hearty breakfast already—so this is not as easy as it looks. If teams choose Forge, they will be heading across the street to a historic site where teams will learn how a blacksmith once functioned. There each team member must make a set of horseshoes.

[HEATHER and MICHELLE enter.]

MICHELLE: Heather, we're going with Forge.

HEATHER: But Michelle, I've never worked with wood before!

MICHELLE: *[frustrated]* Are you kidding me? Horseshoes are made of metal, not wood.

HEATHER: Oh. So we have to make three whole horseshoes?

MICHELLE: We have to make a full set. That would be *four.* How many horses do you know with only three feet?

HEATHER: You don't have to be so rude!

MICHELLE: You don't have to be so dumb! Why did I pick you of all people to be my teammate?

HEATHER: Because I'm your sister!

MICHELLE: Yeah, you definitely can't pick your relatives.

[HEATHER and MICHELLE exit.]

FRANK: Heather and Michelle head to the blacksmith to make the horseshoes. Uriah and Joy were ahead of them.

[URIAH and JOY enter.]

URIAH: All right! Horses! It will be a lot of work, but it might be fun.

JOY: I hope I figure out how to do this. What if my arms aren't strong enough? What if we fall behind the other teams?

URIAH: Don't think about the race. Just focus on this one task and you'll be fine. You're strong. I know you can do it.

JOY: You're right. We can do it together, Uriah. We've already come so far, and we've gotten past so many obstacles. We'll do it as a team just as we've done this whole race.

URIAH: Let's get to work!

[URIAH and JOY exit. While FRANK begins his next line, CRAIG and BEN enter with two chairs in hand and sit down, facing audience, as if sitting at a restaurant table. Or if you choose to have the real food, CRAIG and BEN should be seated at the table with the plates of food already in front of them.]

FRANK: Craig and Ben are the only team to go with Gorge. The Roost serves up the two guys with their first of seven heaping plates of the Sunrise Sampler.

BEN: I'm always hungry. Craig, we can do this task in no time.

CRAIG: If you say so. But I'm a little nervous about this food.

[CRAIG and BEN pantomime eating food or begin eating it.]

BEN: Wow. You're right. This food does taste bad! *[yells, looking around]* Hey, who cooked this junk anyway?!

CRAIG: Ben! Why are you always mean?

BEN: I'm not mean. They're mean for cooking this stuff and calling it food! Here, I know how we can get around this. Drop a little on the floor. *[pantomimes dropping food or really do it]* Stuff some more in your napkin. *[pantomimes hiding food in napkin or really do it]*

CRAIG: But Ben, that's cheating!

BEN: It's all about winning the prize money. I don't care what I have to do to get it.

[CRAIG and BEN continue to pantomime talking and eating as FRANK says his last line.]

FRANK: After teams finish their detour, they will get another clue. They must travel eight miles north by bus to the next pit stop. The last team to check in there *may* be eliminated. Who will arrive first? Who will pull together as a team to take the lead on the next leg of the journey? Find out when we come back, here on *The Attitude Race*.

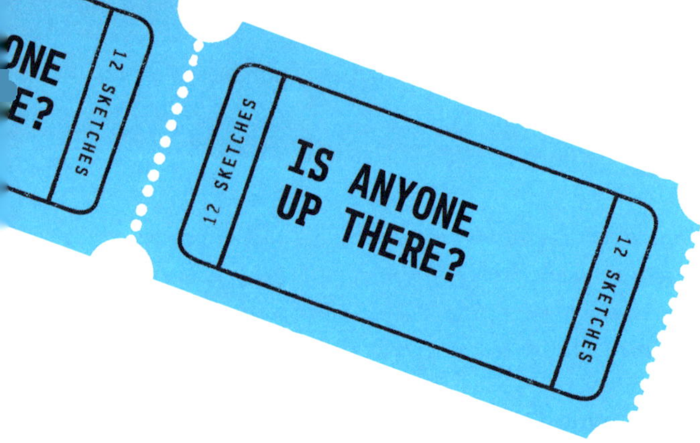

>>> **PURPOSE:**

Use this skit to introduce a discussion about how people can draw
closer to God through prayer.

>>> **POSSIBLE SCRIPTURES:**

Matthew 6:9-13

Matthew 7:7-12

>>> **PROPS:**

none

>>> **PEOPLE:**

KELLY—prom queen type

STAN—jock

NICK—future rock star

NINA—holier-than-thou type

ELLA—shopaholic

MAX—sincerely good guy

Each character is on the stage throughout the entire skit. They should be spaced out at various places across the stage with their heads bowed, arms to side until it's their turn to speak. Then they should look up and begin. When they are finished, they should go back to heads bowed, arms to side.

KELLY: Hi, God, it's me, Kelly. Let me just start by saying, I'm really glad you made me good-looking. I mean, I look at my brother and think, *Wow, close call!* Now, about this homecoming dance. I'd like to put an order in for Jay Johnson as a date. Mmmm, he is fine! If you can't get him, which I know you can because you can do anything, try Blake Sinclair because he's pretty popular and he's on the basketball team. Whatever you do, make sure I don't have any major breakouts before pictures. I wasn't too thrilled with my yearbook photo. So there you have it, Lord. Just remember: Jay Johnson . . . big dance . . . no zits. And PS: Don't let Stan ask me out, because he is *such* a loser. Amen.

STAN: Hey, Lord, Stan here. You know, the football player. I know I haven't talked to you in quite a while. Actually, I guess it was, like, Vacation Bible School, when I was seven. Man, I was really great in Little League that summer. We've got a big game coming up, homecoming, and you have to help us win. And if you don't mind, could I catch the winning pass? Because I'm planning on asking Kelly to homecoming and that would really impress her. So there you have it, Lord. Just remember: winning pass . . . Kelly . . . big dance . . . hubba hubba! Over and out.

NICK: Hey, what's up, God? It's Nick. The band voted, and they picked me to talk to you about this. We've got a deal for you. We wanna be rock stars. And in exchange, when we're super-famous, we'll attend church every other Sunday and one Wednesday a month . . . except while we're touring. So do we have a deal or what? Let me know. Later.

NINA: My Father, which art in Heaven, thou art infinitely abundant in goodness whilst we art humble before thee. Rainest down fire upon the wicked Mrs. Waverly, for she didst not select thy devoted and most talented servant, me, Nina, at cheerleading tryouts. For thou art truly a God of justice, and I am truly most deserving. In thy great name I prayest, Ahhhhhmen.

ELLA: Where have you been? I asked you specifically to help me on that math test I had to take, and when I got in there, I didn't know any of the answers. I probably flunked. I know I didn't study, but there was that great sale on leather boots at the mall, and I know how important it is to you that I spend money wisely. So just make sure I pass, OK? Yours truly, Ella.

MAX: God? Are you up there? It's me, Max. I need to talk. I messed up again. Thanks for forgiving me again and again. I don't mean to be greedy. I just need your grace so much. I want to try harder to honor you. Amen.

Use this skit to introduce a discussion about why Jesus is reliable and why we should put our trust in him.

John 8:12-30

John 10:30-38

two cell phones

MOM

CHRIS

MOM and CHRIS stand on opposite sides of the stage, each on the phone, as if they are in two separate places.

MOM: Hello?

CHRIS: Hey, Mom.

MOM: Chris, where have you been? I expected you home an hour ago.

CHRIS: I'm still at the mall. I had a little trouble . . .

MOM: Trouble? Are you OK?

CHRIS: I'm fine, Mom. Just a little car trouble.

MOM: That car of yours!

CHRIS: I know, I know. But it's really a good car.

MOM: Good car! This is the fifth time in two weeks that it stopped running on you! What is it now? Won't start? Another flat tire? That awful black smoke? Oh, *please* don't tell me the engine caught on fire again!

CHRIS: It's OK. *Really.* I just think I'm out of gas.

MOM: You *think* you're out of gas? You don't know?

CHRIS: Well the gas gauge stopped working last week.

MOM: Chris!

CHRIS: And I let Robby borrow it yesterday. He promised to fill it up for me, but I don't think that happened.

MOM: Robby? Haven't I told you that you can't count on Robby for anything?

[CHRIS has trouble hearing his mom, so he starts walking around, trying to get reception.]

CHRIS: Mom? You're cutting out on me here. My cell phone doesn't always work right in the mall. Let me step outside.

[CHRIS takes a couple of steps to the side.]

MOM: Chris, are you still there?

CHRIS: Yeah. That's clearer. Can you help me?

MOM: Sure. I'll send your dad right over. You missed dinner though. Have you eaten?

Chris: No. I'm kind of starved.

Mom: Give dad time to stop for some gas for you and swing by a drive-through and grab you a burger.

Chris: Thanks. By the way . . .

Mom: Yes?

Chris: There are a couple video games here that I really gotta have. Could Dad buy those for me while he's here?

Mom: I don't think so. Not tonight.

Chris: Mom! Can't I count on you guys for *anything*?

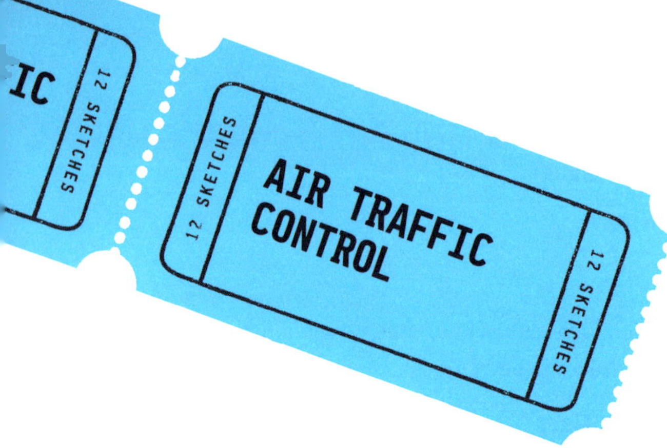

Use this skit to introduce a discussion about our emotions—how they can get away from us and how we can give them over to God's control. (This skit looks at fear, but it can lead into a discussion of other emotions as well.)

Psalm 42
Psalm 73

four to eight chairs
piece of paper folded like a pamphlet
briefcase

Captain—voice only
Harriet Schrapnel—nervous and afraid of flying
Noah Shurance—annoyingly calm in all situations

Flight Attendant—nonspeaking role

Other Plane Passengers (two to four)—nonspeaking roles

The chairs should be set up to look like rows of airplane seats, facing straight ahead or angled toward the audience. Harriet and Noah should be seated together on the front row on the right side of the "plane," with Harriet at the "window." Noah should have the pamphlet in the briefcase, with the briefcase stored under his seat. Other Plane Passengers may fill the others seats and can react and pantomime talking to one another as the Captain makes his announcements. The Captain should speak his lines offstage (into a microphone or just loudly backstage or even in the audience).

Captain: Please fasten your seat belts and put your tray tables in the upright position.

Harriet: *[nervously]* Um, hi. I'm Harriet Schrapnel.

Noah: *[businesslike]* I'm Noah. Noah Shurance. Glad to meet you. *[shakes Harriet's hand]*

Harriet: *[jittery, pretends to look out window]* Wow . . . whew, we're already up in the air. Have you flown over an ocean before?

Noah: You seem a little nervous. First flight?

Harriet: I wish! No, I'm always a wreck when I fly!

Noah: Too bad. You should attend one of my seminars.

Captain: *[very cheery]* Good morning, folks. I'd like to welcome you to Air Airlines. I'm your captain today on our nonstop flight to London. We'll soon be cruising at an altitude of 50,000 feet at the speed of 500 miles an hour with an outside temperature of 50 below, over the deepest part of the Atlantic ocean with no land in sight for another six hours and just b-a-a-rely enough fuel to get there. Oh, and we'll have about 100 percent chance of turbulence along the way! So sit back, relax, and enjoy the ride!

Harriet: So what kind of seminar do you teach?

Noah: It's called "Get a Grip and Get a Life." I'm speaking in London tomorrow night. You should come. It would do you a world of good.

Harriet: Oh really? I've never heard of you before. Do people actually . . . come to your seminars?

NOAH: Oh, you'd be surprised at how many people don't know how to get ahold of reality in a crisis. *[points out the window]* Ah, just look at those clouds. Aren't they spectacular?

HARRIET: *[distracted]* Uh, sure . . . nice. *[looks out window again]* Oh no! Is that smoke coming out of one of the engines? Noah, can you see that smoke?!

NOAH: *[calmly]* Hmm, you're right. It looks like smoke. *[calls back behind him down the airplane aisle]* Excuse me, flight attendant? Flight attendant? [FLIGHT ATTENDANT *enters from rear and goes to see what* NOAH *wants.]* I believe one of the engines may be on fire. You might want to notify the captain. *[trying to be funny]* You could just say, "Houston, we have a problem." Heh, heh.

[FLIGHT ATTENDANT *exits to go to front of plane.* OTHER PLANE PASSENGERS *can react to* NOAH *and* HARRIET *as they hear them.]*

HARRIET: We're all gonna die!!!

NOAH: *[nicely]* Well, Ms. Schrapnel, life *is* terminal. We are all going to die at some point. Excuse me, I have to make a call. *[pretends to reach for the plane phone that would be above the tray table in front of him]* While I call, you can take a look at this. *[pulls his briefcase from under his seat, opens it to get out the pamphlet paper and hands the paper to* HARRIET*]*

HARRIET: What's this?

NOAH: A handout from my seminar.

HARRIET: *[talking to herself]* I can't believe this is happening. I know—I'll find a parachute and right before we crash I'll push open the escape hatch. *[calls out, looking around]* Hey, anybody got a parachute? Anyone? $50 cash! *[no one responds; talks to herself again]* OK fine! Just fine! . . . Wait! I know! The seat cushions! When people stand up to escape, I can get a whole bunch of seat cushions and strap them together with these headphone cords and make a raft. Then I can hurl myself into the sea.

NOAH: *[pretends to talk into phone, very calmly and nonchalant]* Hi, honey. Yeah, everything's fine. But it does look like our plane may be going down. Yes, that's right. The engine appears to be on fire. That's right. By the way, the car is due for an oil change, in case I don't get back. Tell the kids I love them. Bye. *[hangs up the phone]*

HARRIET: *[getting frustrated]* The plane's going down, we're all going to die, and your feathers aren't even ruffled! Are you crazy?!

NOAH: Crazy? No, don't think so. Are *you* crazy?

HARRIET: I'm not crazy. I just don't want to die—not like this!

NOAH: Just how *do* you want to die, Harriet? Car accident? Dreaded disease? Murder, old age, starving to death in a Turkish prison? *[cheerfully]* Actually, as deaths go, this one isn't too bad—quick with lots of media coverage.

HARRIET: *[enraged]* How can you not feel *anything*?!

NOAH: Oh, I am feeling everything you are feeling—fear, uncertainty, anger, sadness. I'm just managing my feelings. It's all outlined in my book on anger, *Adrenaline and You*, and in my latest lecture series on grief management, which I'm calling "Cry Me a River—Then Lend Me Your Jet Ski."

HARRIET: I can't take it anymore!

NOAH: *[still calm]* You and several billion others. This is why my seminar is so popular.

CAPTAIN: This is the captain speaking. No cause for alarm about that right engine, folks, just some high-level condensation and what's left of a flock of birds. Lunch will be served soon, and then we'll start our in-flight movie.

HARRIET: So we're not going to die?

NOAH: Better call my wife back. I *can* do that oil change after all.

This skit is a parody of a clean-up-and-reorganize-your-house type of show (so it requires more props than usual!). Use it to introduce a discussion about materialism and our attitudes toward possessions.

1 Chronicles 29:10-20

Ecclesiastes 5:10, 11

Malachi 3:6-10

Luke 12:16-21

1 Timothy 6:17-19

a container holding several bottles of nail polish

a few fancy dresses draped over a chair

five pairs of shoes

a medium-size box that will hold a few pairs of shoes

an old figurine (some knickknack that would sit on a shelf)

three signs labeled: "Keep," "Trash," "Sell"

(optional) camera

(optional) other stuff that would normally clutter a teen girl's room
(ex: books, papers, CDs, clothes, makeup, hair products, etc.)

TAMARA—TV host who is enthusiastic
NOELLE—teen whose room is overwhelmed with stuff
PARKER—organizer who is nice yet firm in getting his job done

TAMARA should begin her first lines to the audience offstage or in the audience itself and then move onstage, which will be in NOELLE's room. NOELLE's room can already be set up with NOELLE in it as TAMARA gives her opening line. All the items should be scattered around NOELLE's room. Just make sure the characters know where the specific items are that will be discussed later in the skit. The "Keep," "Trash," and "Sell" signs should sit on the floor to indicate three piles of items—the signs should be folded so that they stand up to be seen by audience.

TAMARA: Welcome to another episode of *Clean Your Room*, the show where we clear the clutter from your crazy spaces. I'm your host, Tamara. Today we'll be visiting Noelle, a teen whose bedroom is out of control! Let's check it out. *[moves onstage to see NOELLE's room]* So, Noelle, your dad nominated you for this bedroom makeover?

NOELLE: *[laughing a bit]* Yeah. He threatened to declare it a disaster area if I didn't clean it up. I really do try, but life gets busy, and putting things away isn't my first priority.

TAMARA: Yes, we can see!

NOELLE: My dad, he figured I might need a little outside help.

TAMARA: That's why we're here. Noelle, as you know, to get this process started, we need to meet Parker, organizer extraordinaire!

[PARKER enters.]

PARKER: Hi, Noelle. Glad to meet you.

TAMARA: Parker will be helping you through the process of looking at your stuff and seeing what you don't really need. I'll leave you in his capable hands.

[TAMARA exits.]

PARKER: Now that we take a close look at all your things, it seems a bit overwhelming, doesn't it?

NOELLE: Yeah. I never realized just how much stuff I had!

PARKER: That can happen to anyone, even teenagers. We always want more, and we keep holding on to what we've got. That's why this part of the process may be the most difficult for you. We are going to make three piles—Keep, Trash, and Sell. *[indicates signs on the floor]* You can only have a limited amount in the Keep pile. The things that can be sold, you will put in the Sell pile, and you'll be pricing them later with Tamara for a yard sale. The things that aren't worth selling will go to the Trash pile. Are you ready?

NOELLE: I think. It might be kind of hard. I'm pretty attached to my things.

PARKER: That's why I'm here to help you out.

NOELLE: OK. Let's start.

PARKER: All right. *[picks up the container of nail polish]* Now these items look as if they'll go in the trash pile.

NOELLE: My toenail polish collection? What if I need them?

PARKER: You don't have enough toes to necessitate 50 colors of polish.

NOELLE: Well, shouldn't I try to sell them in the yard sale?

PARKER: I don't think anyone would want to purchase half-used bottles of polish that have touched someone else's feet.

NOELLE: I guess you're right. *[takes container from PARKER and puts beside "Trash" sign]*

PARKER: But over here . . . *[points to the fancy dresses which are laid over a chair; picks up one as he speaks]* These items would be marvelous for a yard sale.

NOELLE: Oh! All my homecoming dresses. Do I have to get rid of them?

PARKER: Every female I meet keeps her fancy dresses, thinking that she'll wear them again someday. Trust me, you won't. By the way, how many homecoming dances did you go to with all of these dresses? *[sorts through the pile]* You're only a junior in high school!

NOELLE: Well, I went to two dances last year—one was at my school and one was with a friend at his school. And then a couple of those I bought but didn't end up wearing.

PARKER: There is such a thing as a return policy, you know.

NOELLE: Yeah, I just couldn't make up my mind in time.

PARKER: When you go in a store, try to determine that you will only purchase an item you know you like. Too many people think, *Oh, I'll just return it if I don't like it,* and then never do, like you. You can sell these dresses in the yard sale.

NOELLE: I know some other girls will enjoy them.

[NOELLE moves the entire chair with the pile of dresses over to the "Sell" sign.]

PARKER: OK, next let's consider your shoes.

NOELLE: I don't know how I could ever *live* without any of my shoes!

PARKER: We're trying to cut back on excess here. Take a good look at your shoes and see what you really wear on a regular basis. Think of what you truly *need. [hands NOELLE the box]* Here's a container—I will let you keep as many shoes as you can fit in here, but no more.

NOELLE: I like them all! How do I choose? Well, OK, I don't really need these, I guess. *[puts one pair of shoes in the Sell pile]* These will be good for school. *[puts a pair of shoes in the box]* These can go—they don't even fit right. *[puts another pair of shoes in the Sell pile]* And I need these and these. *[puts two more pairs of shoes in the box]* OK. These are the ones I'm keeping.

PARKER: Good work! Now let's consider all the knickknacks you have decorating your room. *[picks up figurine]* What about this figurine?

NOELLE: *[takes figurine from PARKER]* My grandmother gave me that when I was 4 years old.

PARKER: But you're not 4 any longer.

NOELLE: I know, but I think of her when I see it.

PARKER: Now I know it has sentimental value. But it's just taking up space and gathering dust. Remember, this is just a gift from your grandmother. It is not actually your grandmother herself. That may sound odd, but sometimes we attach so many emotions to the item itself when it's really the person that we care about.

NOELLE: I never thought about all that.

PARKER: Here's an idea—why don't I take a picture of you holding the figurine? That way you can get rid of it, but you can keep the picture to treasure the memory.

NOELLE: I guess that might work. I hardly ever look at the figurine anymore, but it would be nice to remember it.

PARKER: Now you're talking. *[picks up camera or can pantomime taking her picture]* OK. Just pose really quickly. Big smile. *[takes or pantomimes taking her picture]* And there you go.

NOELLE: Wow. There's still so much stuff left. How will I ever go through it all? I never realized I liked having so many things. There are movie posters, my scented lotion collection, more makeup than I ever wear, jewelry, purses, not to mention all my CDs and DVDs. Why do I even have all this?

PARKER: That's just how our society works. We define ourselves by our things. It's OK to have things, but sometimes they rule our lives instead of making our lives better.

[TAMARA enters again and goes to her opening spot offstage or in the audience to deliver the last line. PARKER and NOELLE continue to pantomime talking and going through her stuff.]

TAMARA: I think Noelle is learning a few life lessons through this process, don't you? As Parker helps Noelle finish with the rest of her things, we'll take a break for a commercial. When we get back, Noelle and I will tackle the yard sale! See you in a few!

Use this skit to introduce a discussion about how we can honor God through our jobs and through working hard at any task we do.

Ephesians 6:5-9

Colossians 3:22-24

matching brightly colored shirts as OLIVIA and LARRY's work uniforms

table or something to be a fast-food counter

piece of foil or paper that looks like a burger wrapper

OLIVIA—employee of McTaco Hut

CUSTOMER—can be male or female

LARRY—assistant manager of McTaco Hut

OLIVIA stands behind the table or other object representing the fast-food counter. She looks bored. CUSTOMER enters, carrying the foil or paper wrapper.

OLIVIA: *[runs this entire sentence together in a monotone voice, sounding bored]* Welcome to McTaco Hut my name is Olivia how can I help you?

CUSTOMER: *[holds up foil or paper wrapper]* I just filled out this employment application I found on the wrapper of my burrito burger.

OLIVIA: Hold on. You don't want to work here.

CUSTOMER: Why not?

OLIVIA: Are you kidding? Look at this uniform. Have you ever seen anything this hideous?

CUSTOMER: It is kind of . . . bright.

OLIVIA: Bright!? I have to plug it in when I'm at the counter, and it has a battery pack that weighs a ton. You know, I risk electrocution every time I mop the floor.

CUSTOMER: I was just in the restroom, so I'd guess *that's* not a big concern for you.

OLIVIA: You know it! If it weren't for the assistant manager, I'd only mop the floor once a week. He makes me mop the whole place at least three times a week! What a jerk!

CUSTOMER: *[surprised and disgusted]* Three times a week? That's ALL?! Yuck! I take it he's on vacation this week.

OLIVIA: No, he's here, why?

CUSTOMER: Well, I just had to peel my shoe off the floor in that booth over there. Anyway, the application says I should give it to a manager. Could I speak with him?

OLIVIA: Don't say I didn't warn you. Hey, Larry! There's someone who filled out an application.

[LARRY enters.]

LARRY: Hi, I'm Larry, the assistant manager. Do you have a moment for a quick interview?

[LARRY guides CUSTOMER over to another part of the stage, away from OLIVIA and the counter. OLIVIA continues to stand and look bored.]

CUSTOMER: Sure, I really need a job.

LARRY: That's great! We're kind of shorthanded these days. Our manager has been firing people right and left over the past few weeks.

CUSTOMER: Why are so many people getting fired?

LARRY: The woman is impossible to work for. Just last week, Olivia and I were racing mop buckets and we bumped into Jerry. He dropped his battery pack into the fryer and set three drive-through orders on fire. It was really cool!

CUSTOMER: Then what happened?

LARRY: The manager came around the corner and saw Jerry fishing around in the fryer with a mop, trying to get his battery pack out. I just started yelling at Olivia to clean up the mess and grabbed a fire extinguisher and put out the fire.

CUSTOMER: Wow, that was quick thinking.

LARRY: I'll say. Jerry took the fall for that one. That was almost as close a call as when she nearly caught us playing cards in the walk-in freezer. I really miss Jerry. He could take orders, make orders, and make *correct* change faster than anyone.

CUSTOMER: It sounds like he was a really good worker.

LARRY: Yeah, he was. I was sort of training him to be *my* assistant. I'd let him handle the complaint calls we got and check the registers for me at the end of the shift. In fact, I'd let him wear my assistant manager badge whenever I needed to "step out" for a few minutes.

CUSTOMER: Well, it sounds like there's a place for me here.

LARRY: Hey, do you think you could replace Jerry?

CUSTOMER: Not exactly. Could I speak to *your* manager?

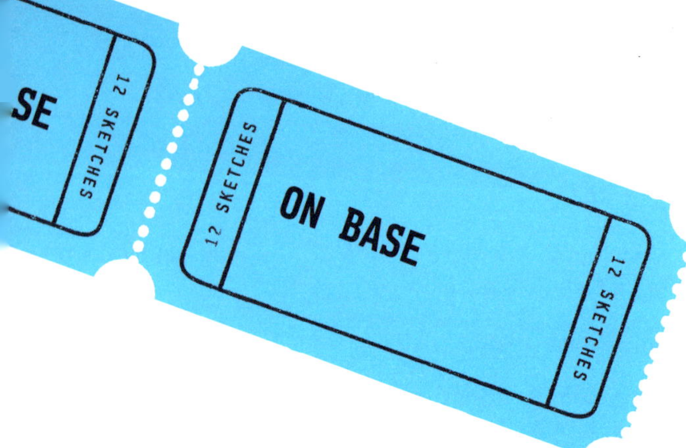

Use this sports show skit to discuss where we can place our confidence—people disappoint us, but God is in control and we are secure in him.

2 Timothy 1:11-14

2 Timothy 2:1, 2

table or desk

chair

papers

suit for JOHN TRACE to wear

JOHN—host of a TV sports show

DALE—sports fan

SOPHIE—a mom whose son is a huge sports fan

BRADY—president of a fan club

Begin with JOHN, wearing a suit, sitting in a chair behind a table or desk, set up like a sports show host would be. JOHN has papers in front of him that he can shuffle and look at occasionally during the sketch. When all other characters enter, they should be on another part of the stage, facing the audience as they talk—as if they are speaking to the host, JOHN, on camera, live via satellite.

JOHN: *[can look at papers in front of him occasionally as a TV anchor would]* Hello, and welcome to *On Base with John Trace,* your place to discuss the latest baseball news. I'm your host, John Trace. Of course, the big story of the day concerns the reports swirling about former All-Star outfielder, Austin Holbrook. As Austin and his wife are in a bitter divorce fight, a picture of Holbrook is emerging that is quite different from the fan favorite of the past decade. Holbrook had the reputation of being a family man with impeccable credentials. He was an outspoken advocate of clean play on the field and clean living off the field. But now we are hearing testimony of a very different nature. We sent our camera crew to Holbrook's hometown of Springfield to see what fans have to say. We'll talk to them live via satellite. First up we have Dale.

[DALE enters stage and stands where all three "via satellite" characters will speak.]

JOHN: Dale, you're *On Base with John Trace.*

DALE: Thanks, John.

JOHN: So Dale, what do you think of these allegations?

DALE: I'm really shocked. Do you think the charges of Austin cheating on his wife are true? I mean, she could have just made it up to get a bigger divorce settlement.

JOHN: Well, Dale, I wish that Austin's wife just made it up. But my friends down at the courthouse tell me that a lot of women have come forward with basically the same story.

DALE: Oh, man . . .

JOHN: I feel your pain, Dale. Let's talk to someone else.

[DALE exits. SOPHIE enters and stands where DALE was standing.]

JOHN: Now we hear from Sophie, a concerned mother. Sophie, you're *On Base with John Trace.*

SOPHIE: *[hesitantly]* John?

JOHN: Go ahead, Sophie, you're on the air.

SOPHIE: John, I have an 8-year-old son who idolized Austin. He had all of his baseball cards and a big poster of him in his room.

JOHN: So what do you think of Holbrook now?

SOPHIE: I always admired Austin because of his stance against using drugs and alcohol. I figured if my son was going to have a hero, who better? But Austin went against everything he said he believed. I've lost my trust in him.

JOHN: So the stories about the possible steroid use, all-night drinking binges, and parties are a problem for you?

SOPHIE: And for my son. John, you've never seen a sadder face on a kid than when he found out. And the next day the poster was torn down and I found his baseball cards in the trash.

JOHN: Ouch! That really hurts. Who do we have up next?

[SOPHIE exits. BRADY enters and stands where SOPHIE was standing.]

BRADY: Hey, John. I'm Brady, and I'm president of the Austin Holbrook Fan Club here in Springfield.

JOHN: Hey, Brady. So what's the reaction from Holbrook's biggest fans?

BRADY: John, you wouldn't believe the e-mails I'm getting from club members. We've had almost a 20 percent loss in membership in the past day.

JOHN: Wow. So what is making the fans the angriest?

BRADY: It's not just one charge. It's the whole scandal. More than any other player, Austin always seemed to be above it all. You know. When baseball was at its worst, we could always say, "Hey, there's always Austin" or "They're not all like that. Holbrook still stands for what the game is all about."

JOHN: But not anymore?

Brady: Not anymore. I mean if we can't even count on Austin Holbrook, who can we count on?

John: Good question. *[to audience]* In just a few minutes, we'll talk to some more fans and see if anyone has some answers. We'll be back after we break for a word from our sponsors.

Use this skit to introduce a discussion about trusting God when we feel anxious or worried.

Matthew 6:25-34

Luke 12:22-31

Philippians 4:6

seven chairs

HELGA SCHMIDELTON—leader of the support group; she's overly peppy in trying to get everyone involved

HENRY—has the most worries of the group members

SYDNEY

CARL

LILY

ED

ISAAC

All characters have irrational worries. Each cast member can find a quirky way to display these fearful qualities. The chairs should be set up in a half circle to show a support group setting but so that no backs are facing the audience. At the beginning of the scene, people should be standing around the stage, talking to one another in pairs or small groups.

Helga: All right now, folks, let's each take a seat and start our sharing time.

[Everyone sits down.]

Helga: *[very cheery]* Welcome to the Anxiety Support Group. I'm Helga Schmidelton, your group leader, and I applaud your courage for being here! You are facing your worries—those horrible, nightmarish imaginings that frazzle your nerves and threaten to wring the very life from you! Now, well, we shall begin as usual, by going around the circle and sharing in turn one thing we tend to worry about. Often just talking it out dispels the shadows in our minds.

Henry: *[nervous, brooding]* I don't like shadows. Frightening things, shadows. When I was a kid, I had this rocking chair in my room, and when I threw clothes over the back, it cast a shadow. At night . . . in the dark . . . it looked like the Hunchback of Notre Dame.

Helga: *[patiently]* Yes, Henry, well, thank you for your contribution. We'll come around to you in a moment. *[clears throat]* Shall we begin on my left with Sydney?

Sydney: *[uncertainly]* Um . . . it sounds a little silly saying it out loud . . .

Helga: It's perfectly all right, Sydney. We're not here to judge, are we, folks?

[Everyone mutters halfheartedly.]

Helga: *[cheerfully ignores the mutters]* See, we're all behind you!

Henry: Don't you hate it when people sneak up behind you and go, "Boo!"? I'm always afraid that will happen in a cafeteria when I have a tray full of food and all my food will go—

Helga: *[cuts Henry off]* Thank you for sharing, Henry. Let's let Sydney finish now.

Sydney: Well . . . I'm . . . *[says meekly and quietly]* I'm afraid of getting mauled by a lion on the way to school.

Helga: Why, that would be a frightening thing, wouldn't it? Terrifying! All that blood . . . gore! Well now. Good. Let's go on. Carl?

Carl: I'm worried that my hair will fall out.

Helga: *[after a long pause]* To be honest, your hair does look like it could be, well, thinning.

Carl: Not the hair on my head! My nose hair! I'm afraid my nose hair will fall out. And then when I breathe, all the pollutants in the air will go right to my lungs because there's no nose hair to stop them, and then I'll choke to death!

Helga: Ah yes, of course. I do see your concern. A frightful thing, choking to death. A worry I struggle with myself. I don't wear neck scarves for that very reason. The cutting off of the air, the blackness closing in— *[she gives a little gasp, then gets back to the group]* All right. Lily, I believe you're next?

Lily: *[says her line very quickly]* I'm just going to say that sometimes I'm afraid that my head is going to roll off my shoulders and hit the floor!

Helga: That's very interesting, Lily. A common worry actually! I believe it was the great composer Tchaikovsky who had that very same fear.

Lily: *[hopefully]* Really? I do play the piano!

Henry: Hey, I used to play the piano too, but once I was trying to move one and it rolled over my foot, and ever since then I've been afraid of pianos.

Helga: *[getting frustrated]* Henry, your sharing is very helpful. But *please* wait your turn! Now go ahead, Ed.

Ed: My greatest fear is that a tube of crazy glue will explode in my pocket and my underwear will get stuck to my favorite pants.

Helga: I sympathize with your concern, Ed. Of course, though, the chances of that are so very slim—

Ed: Oh, it already happened once. I'm just afraid it will happen again!

Helga: I see. Isaac, your turn.

Isaac: My worry is that I'll wreck my parents' car and they'll make me take my bike to the prom, which is a really dumb and stupid thing to worry about because I don't even drive yet and I'm not going to the prom because I can't find a date!

Helga: That's all right, Isaac. Don't judge yourself. Now, everyone, remember we mustn't judge ourselves. *[weary sigh as Henry raises his hand]* Henry, you're raising your hand?

Henry: Yeah. I just wanted to say I was judged once. He had a black robe and beady eyes! He looked just like a giant vulture ready to swoop down on me!

Helga: *[sounds tired]* Thank you, Henry. As *always*, thanks for sharing. *[cheerfully again]* Now where were we? Oh yes, we're going to go through our confidence statements next. Stand up and repeat after me: *[Everyone stands.]* "I am bold. I am brave. I am stomping my worries to the ground." *[stomps her foot during the last sentence]*

All Group Members: *[They speak quietly, hesitantly, and generally not bold or brave at all.]* I am bold. I am brave. I am stomping my worries to the ground. *[They don't stomp confidently either, and one person may trip and fall when trying to stomp.]*

Helga: *[excited]* Oh, you've all improved so much from last week! Let's take a restroom break, and when we return, we'll practice our breathing exercises!

Use this skit to introduce a discussion about seeking God's will and direction for life.

Psalm 119:33-40

Psalm 119:97-104

two chairs

table or desk to be the cashier counter

magazine

cell phone or real phone to sit on cashier counter

SADIE—sister of Hunter

HUNTER—brother of Sadie

BROOKE—cashier at gas station

SADIE and HUNTER sit in two chairs side by side on one side of the stage, pretending as if they're in a car, HUNTER driving. BROOKE stands behind a table on the other side of the stage to simulate standing behind the counter of a gas station convenience store. BROOKE is flipping through a magazine and doesn't pay much attention to HUNTER's questions through most of the skit.

SADIE: *[arms folded across chest in frustration]* So?

HUNTER: Sadie, we're not lost.

SADIE: I knew I should have driven! Mom's gonna kill us if we're late! Hunter, just because you're older doesn't mean you always have to drive. You're horrible with directions! We're totally lost!

HUNTER: *[contemplating]* How would you define lost?

SADIE: How? This situation. Us, right now—we are the definition of lost.

HUNTER: *[trying to play off the bad situation]* See, I've always thought that being lost isn't really not knowing where you are, but not knowing what's around you.

SADIE: Do you want to tell the cashier that we're lost, or do you want me to?

HUNTER: We're not lost.

SADIE: *[pretends to start to get out of the car]* I guess she'll probably figure it out when I ask for directions, don't you think?

HUNTER: *[getting desperate]* No, wait. Um . . . I'll go. I'll do it. I don't want you misrepresenting our situation. You pump.

SADIE: Fine.

[SADIE pantomimes getting out of the car and beginning to pump gas. She continues as HUNTER and BROOKE talk. HUNTER pantomimes getting out of the car and opening a door to go into the store. He wanders around, pretending to look at store items and then slowly approaches the counter. BROOKE doesn't pay any attention to him but reads her magazine. HUNTER waits for a moment, then starts a conversation with BROOKE.]

HUNTER: Hi there.

BROOKE: *[doesn't look up from the magazine and speaks as if distracted]* Hi.

HUNTER: Nice day, eh?

Brooke: *[still looking at magazine]* Gorgeous.

Hunter: *[enthusiastically]* My sister is pumping the gas. I'm going to pay when she's done.

Brooke: *[sarcastically]* Super. I'm happy for you.

Hunter: Long shift, huh?

Brooke: *[still looking at magazine]* Uh-huh.

Hunter: You must be pretty tired when you get done. How far of a drive is it to where you live?

Brooke: *[looks up from magazine suspiciously]* Not far.

Hunter: Twenty minutes?

Brooke: Fifteen.

Hunter: What city do you live in?

Brooke: I'm sure you've never heard of it.

Hunter: Oh, try me.

Brooke: It's a small town.

Hunter: Well, I'm pretty familiar with the area. I've got relatives everywhere around here. You might know some of them.

Brooke: Rock Hollow.

Hunter: *[confused, but doesn't want to let on]* What do you mean by that?

Brooke: That's my town. Population 281 . . . unless Ellie Donalds had her baby.

Hunter: Oh sure. Rock Hollow. Yeah. Wow, I hope you have sunglasses—you must be driving straight into the sun.

Brooke: It depends if I'm going to or from work. Either way, I can deal with it.

Hunter: You're a trooper. I'm on my way to Parkersburg. I hope to get there by five o'clock. Do you think I'll make it?

Brooke: I don't know. Or care.

Hunter: Oh, maybe that's because you've got no stake in it. I'll bet you $5 I get there by 5:00.

Brooke: I don't believe in gambling, and there's really no way I'd be able to prove if you got there or not.

Hunter: I see. But do you think that would be a safe bet? Maybe not for you, but in general?

Brooke: *[glances outside at car]* With that car, it's hard to say.

Hunter: Take a guess.

[At this point Sadie finishes pantomiming pumping the gas and pantomimes getting back in the car. She sits and waits, still frustrated.]

Brooke: Yes. That'd be a great bet.

Hunter: I see. *[pauses]* A great bet for me or you?

Brooke: *[getting annoyed]* Sir, that will be $30 for the gas.

Hunter: Oh sure. *[looks outside at Sadie sitting in the car]* My sister is finished, I guess. So . . . you probably get a lot of people coming through here on the way to Tucson?

Brooke: Nope.

Hunter: Oh. Yeah, I guess Phoenix is more likely.

Brooke: No.

Hunter: Winslow?

Brooke: No.

[The following lines are exchanged very quickly.]

Hunter: Flagstaff?

Brooke: Nope.

Hunter: Albuquerque?

Brooke: Nuh-uh.

Hunter: Santa Fe?

Brooke: Never.

Hunter: El Paso?

Brooke: No.

Hunter: Amarillo?

Brooke: No.

Hunter: Las Vegas?

Brooke: Not likely.

Hunter: Denver?

Brooke: Nada.

Hunter: Los Angeles?

Brooke: No.

Hunter: Yeah, I suppose on this side of the continental divide, you get more people passing through on their way to the coast.

Brooke: Sometimes. *[impatient]* Is there anything else I can do for you?

Hunter: Uh, yeah. One quick question. I'm a history buff. Do you happen to know if the U.S. acquired this territory in the Mexican War, or was it in the Gadsden Purchase?

Brooke: *[annoyed]* I don't know, but I'll bet you the sheriff does. Do you want me to call him?

Hunter: No no no. That won't be necessary. Thank YOU, though. *[starts to walk out]* What county's sheriff would you call?

[Brooke pulls out her cell phone or picks up the counter phone and begins to dial.]

Hunter: That's OK. Don't worry about it.

[Hunter heads back to the car and pantomimes closing the door.]

Brooke: Did you find out how to get there?

Hunter: Of course! Look up in the sky right there. Is that the Big Dipper?

Brooke: Hunter, it's daytime.

Hunter: I knew that.

Use this skit to introduce a discussion about the importance of
getting rest.

Psalm 62:5-8

Ecclesiastes 5:12

Matthew 11:28-30

phone with headset or a regular house phone

table

chair

(optional) bed or couch or two chairs put together to serve as a bed

(optional) another phone or cell phone

Operator—male
Caller—female

Operator sits at the desk with the phone sitting in front of him. He can wear a headset if you have one. If there is a button he can hit to make the phone ring, or a sound effect that you can use, it might be fun to do at the beginning of the skit and again at the end when he gets another call. Otherwise, he can just pretend he heard it ring. Operator starts the skit by answering the phone. Option: Caller can either be offstage as voice only or can be on opposite side of stage (as if she's in her house), lying down on the couch or chairs, and talking into a phone.

Operator: *[says this little jingle in a goofy or dramatic way]* Insomniac Hotline! When you can't sleep, we'll have you counting sheep!

Caller: Um hi, how does this thing work exactly?

Operator: You tell me what's bothering you, I evaluate your situation, and then I talk you through some solutions. In no time, you'll be dozing like a baby.

Caller: Do you guarantee results?

Operator: You ever heard of Sleeping Beauty?

Caller: Of course.

Operator: She was our first customer. You can only imagine, after being cursed by a witch and sleeping years of her life away, she wasn't exactly ready to dive right into another nap. But we fixed her right up.

Caller: Wow. I guess if you can help *her,* you can help anyone. Wait a minute. Is there some limited warranty like, "Warning: sleep only guaranteed if customer pricks finger on spinning wheel"?

Operator: No. We've eliminated that clause. Lost too many customers that way. And don't get your hopes too high. Handsome princes are not included. Now let's get down to business. Describe your situation.

Caller: Well, I've been lying here for like three hours, staring at my ceiling in the dark, and I have to get some sleep tonight. There's this big history test I have tomorrow, that I just know I'm gonna flunk, even though I've studied for like a week. It's just that my brain doesn't function well with history, you know? There are all those dates and people and facts, and it all just gets jumbled around in my brain.

OPERATOR: Have you tried those rhyming tricks to remember your history? You know, "In 1492 Columbus sailed the ocean blue"?

CALLER: Who has time to sit around coming up with rhyming stuff when there's so much to do? *[begins to talk faster and faster as she goes through these next lines]* I mean, I get home from school, and already my mom has a list of chores for me. Like take out the garbage, set the table, clean the dishes after dinner, load the dishwasher. Not to mention the other stuff like, *[imitates a mom voice]* "Be a nice sister and spend time with your brother." Yeah, like I wanna spend my entire night playing Candyland. And then Dad tells me to walk the dog: *[imitates a dad voice]* "After all, you're the one who wanted the dog, so you have to be responsible for it." Well the dumb dog somehow got a weird ingrown toenail problem.

OPERATOR: Eww!

CALLER: *[still talking fast]* Tell me about it! Who knew dogs even got such a thing? And so it takes for-ev-er to even walk him around the block. And by that time I barely have enough time to check Facebook before calling Becca to talk about everything that went on at school. There's a lot of news to keep up with these days. Who's dating who, what we're going to wear to Friday's basketball game, why Mrs. Epperson gives us so much math homework—

OPERATOR: Excuse me, ma'am? Exactly how much caffeine have you had today?

CALLER: Not much. Well, not much more than usual. *[speaks fast again]* I had a Red Bull in the morning, to get me jump-started, you know. Gotta start the day off right. And a Mountain Dew at lunch. Then my mom made chocolate cake tonight for dessert. Oh, and Becca and I stopped by the Coffee Bean Café and got a couple of lattes after school.

OPERATOR: OK. Do me a favor and stop for a second. I want you to take a deep breath. Inhale . . .

[CALLER inhales.]

OPERATOR: And exhale.

[CALLER exhales.]

OPERATOR: Good. Now please continue. A bit slower this time.

CALLER: *[tries to speak slower]* So then tonight I can't sleep, and I start thinking and thinking. And all the stuff Becca said just kept running through my head.

OPERATOR: What did she say?

CALLER: She kept talking about her boyfriend and what she should get them for their three-and-a-half day anniversary. *[starts to speed up talking again]* And all I could think about is how I'll never get a guy's attention, let alone a real boyfriend. I'll just be stuck here alone for the rest of my high school life, with only my Justin Timberlake *[or insert name of another pop star]* posters to keep me company. *[tearful]* So by that time I'm depressed enough as it is, not to mention that yesterday at the mall—

OPERATOR: OK! That's enough for now. I think I've got plenty of information to begin the evaluation process. First and foremost, you've GOT to wean yourself away from the Justin posters! The trash can would make a nice new home for them. Second, cut back your caffeine intake by a few lattes. Third, you need to reevaluate your schedule.

[CALLER starts to snore.]

OPERATOR: Are you taking notes? Now the way I see it, you've got to— *[notices snoring]* Hello? Miss? Are you listening?

[CALLER keeps snoring until OPERATOR hangs up the phone.]

OPERATOR: Oh great. It happened again. Just when I'm about to solve all their problems, these teenage girls talk themselves to sleep. Guess I'll save my advice for someone else. *[hangs up phone]*

[Phone instantly rings when he hangs up or else OPERATOR just pretends to hear it ring.]

OPERATOR: Insomniac Hotline! When you can't sleep, we'll have you counting sheep!

Drama can be used in a variety of settings to spark imagination. Here is an example of how we'd use "Read Between the Lines" (page 12) to introduce a devotion about respect. Open your session with the skit. Then make the following devotional presentation:

Disrespect. It kills relationships. Respect, on the other hand—showing genuine esteem or regard for another person—is an essential ingredient for constructing meaningful human relationships. The Bible speaks of a *reason, rights,* and *results* associated with this respect.

REASON ROMANS 13:8
RESPECT IS A DEBT WE OWE OTHERS.

Most of us think about debt as it pertains to money. We owe our friend $5 for the lunch we bought or the bank $5,000 for the car we are buying. We also usually have a plan for paying off any debt we have incurred.

We aren't used to thinking of debts when it comes to our relationships. And there is another twist that God adds here; we are to keep this account open and active as long as we live. We will never be paid in full when it comes to the love and respect we owe others.

Even though we owe it to others, we must remember that we will not automatically receive it. In one of Jesus' parables, a landowner sent his own son to collect from his tenants, thinking they would respect his son simply because of his identity. Instead, he was killed along with the owner's servants (Matthew 21:35-39). Receiving respect is never automatic. Respect, however, can be earned. Scripture teaches that often, if we live a life reflecting God's character, especially marked with kindness, then others will have a tendency to respect us (1 Thessalonians 4:11, 12 and Proverbs 11:16).

Natalie, in our skit, may have excused her disrespect by saying, "I'm just being myself. Miguel needs to accept that." That misses the point. Believers need to begin the process by being the first to accept the "respect debt."

There are at least three reasons most of us will find this to be quite a challenge.

It goes against our nature. Since Adam and Eve, the tendency of human nature is to be selfish. In order for a vehicle to move faster, the driver must shift into a higher gear. In order for us to treat people with respect, we must do the same. The Bible instructs us to be concerned about the interests of others and to work to actively please our neighbor (Philippians 2:4; Romans 15:2). We must shift from the gear of pleasing oneself to the gear of pleasing others.

Making respect a priority in relationships also *goes against our culture.* Most of the voices that both whisper and shout to us encourage us to look out for number one. Media advertising urges the consumer to make personal pleasure the number one motivation of most every purchasing decision. In contrast, God's Word instructs, "Do nothing out of selfish ambition or vain conceit, but in humility consider others better than yourselves (Philippians 2:3).

Finally, living out relationships of respect *requires a different role model.* Many of us elevate and emulate movie and music stars and professional athletes. Many of these same individuals live lives marked by selfishness and disrespect. If we want to see what respect looks like we must focus our attention on someone else—Jesus. In Philippians 2:5 we are told, "Your attitude should be the same as that of Christ Jesus." His attitude was marked by respect, selflessness, humility, and sacrifice (Philippians 2:6-8).

Back to the skit, Natalie may have thought it was her "right" to have her ego fed by flirting with other guys. As innocent as the flirtation might have been, she should have been willing to give up that right to please Miguel.

Let's assume that Natalie went to church every Sunday and prayed regularly, but in relationships with guys she saw them as little more than playthings rather than as people to be treated with respect. We could imagine that she often felt that she wasn't really connecting with God. Perhaps she was receiving the wrong results because of not developing right relationships. In this verse of Scripture God makes it clear that improper treatment in our relationships with others can hinder our communication with him.

We are bombarded with messages about what to respect and not respect. Animal rights activists tell us that it is imperative we respect animals, which they say means it is wrong to eat them, use them for scientific experiments, or wear their skins as clothing. God, on the other hand, has given us control over the animals and even fashioned garments of skins for Adam and Eve after the fall (Genesis 1:28; 3:21). Some environmental activists tell us to respect the earth because it is the source of our existence. God, on the other hand, wants us to love and respect him as creator and serve as caretaker of the glorious creation he has authored (Genesis 1:1; 2:15). It is extremely important to recognize the value God places on people and the need to respect them. It gives him great pleasure when our respect follows his wishes rather than those in the world around us.

If our relationships with others aren't what they should be, one of the first places to check is the issue of respect. Are we valuing others as we should? God has attached a reason, rights, and results to the living out of this important quality.

INDEX BY SCRIPTURE